THE ROAD AHEAD

THE ROAD AHEAD

RENEE GUDEX

yucky papa ink

The Road Ahead
By Renee Gudex
May God bless all who read this story as they walk the journey before them.

All pictures are provided through creative commons or istock and are the property of the original photographers. The story itself is an original work and is the property of the author Renee Gudex

THE ROAD AHEAD - 3

Dear child of God,

You are not alone. God is always here. From your top to your bottom. He created you.

The Journey ahead is long and full of dangers. Sometimes you will feel pain. Sometimes you will feel joy. Somedays you will laugh. Somedays you will cry. Somedays you do both and wont even know why.

But child of God do not be afraid, God will never leave you. He always knows the way.

This Photo by Unknown Author is licensed under CC BY SA

Sometimes you will make mistakes and go the wrong way. When you do just remember: We all do, and God knows it too. That is why he sent Jesus to die for you.

So dust yourself off. Leave the pain at the cross but take the lessons with you. For Christ blood has cleansed you.

Sometimes it wont make sense and you will wonder why? You will ask for an answer and here nothing in reply. You will think he is not their or too busy or you. Your faith will be tested. Your heart will be broken. But child of God do not give up, do not turn around. God is in control and he is holding you.

This Photo by Unknown Author is licensed under CC BY

Every tear you will cry, every pain you will feel. Will not be in vain. His promises are true, and he will always fight for you.

So hold your head up high, and walk the path that you have been given. Always remembering your father in heaven.

His love is patient. His love is unconditional. He will see you at your worst. He will see you at your best, and rest assured he is not afraid of the mess. So come to Jesus as you are, and your faith in him will take you far.

The path you will walk on he has already traveled. He has prepared the road for you.

So get up child of God, and get ready for the amazing adventure God has planned just for you.

Dear god,
Thank you for blessing this world with a person like this.
May you walk with them in their life and bring them to faith in you.
In Jesus name.
Amen

12 - RENEE GUDEX

14 - RENEE GUDEX

www.ingramcontent.com/pod-product-compliance
Lightning Source LLC
Chambersburg PA
CBHW041217070526
44583CB00001B/17